The Song:
PERC
FREN(

CW00500421

by James N. Healy

With the Compliments of
T. Oscar Rollins

OSSIAN

published in association
with Mercier Press

To the Misses Ettie and Joan French who retain such a lively memory of their father and to my late beloved Aunts Rose, May and Theo who were of the same mind and generation. Bless them.

© Mercier Press, Cork,
(originally published as The First Book of Ballads, 1955,
and The Second Book of Ballads, 1962)
Revised edition 1986
© 1996. This edition Ossian Publications Ltd, Cork, Ireland
World Copyright

All rights reserved, including the right of reproduction in
whole or in part in any form or by any means without the
prior permission of the copyright owners. Photocopying
any part of this work is illegal and expressly forbidden by
the Copyright Act of 1956.
Copying is also illogical and short-sighted, as because of it,
authors, composers and arrangers will not receive royalties
for their work, nor will the publishers be able to continue
their job of producing new titles.

Music artwork by Sarah M. Burn, Guitar chords by Ray O'Donoghue
Design by John Loesberg
Cover photo: special thanks to Brendan O'Dowda
Printed by Colour Books, Dublin

OSSIAN PUBLICATIONS LTD.
P.O.Box 84, Cork, Ireland
E Mail: ossian@iol.ie

OMB 115
ISBN 1 900428 25 3

Preface

William Percy French was born at Cloonyquin House, not far from the town of Roscommon, on 1 May 1854. His father was a landlord and his mother came from nearby Carrick-on-Shannon, being the daughter of the Rev. William Percy, rector of the town.

The son of a landlord, and grandson of a clergyman was not the most likely person to become a popular writer of Irish songs considering the times, but that is what young Willie became. (He was not known as 'Percy' until his professional stage days.)

His talent, however, became apparent at an early age as, with his neighbouring friends the Godleys, he was the leading spirit of improvised performances at houses in the district. Later, as a student at Trinity College, this talent developed and it came to full bloom when, on graduation as an engineer, he went to work in Cavan as an 'Inspector of Drains'. This was the period which gave rise to many of his best songs.

When, after seven years, this job ran out he returned to Dublin and, for want of other employment, acted for a period as editor of a magazine called *The Jarvey*, filling in the time with occasional performances which gradually developed into a one-man show. This displayed all his talents, for as well as being a composer and singer of his own songs he had great ability as an artist, basically in water colours, but expressed in his show with 'smoke pictures' on plates, and what became known as 'upside down' pictures.

While telling one of his tongue in cheek stories he continued to sketch with coloured chalk on a large sheet of brown paper, and then, when the story was finished would turn it around, and, to the audience's delight, it would be something else.

In 1891 he met Houston Collisson for the first time, and for many years they formed a partnership, with Collisson supplying much of the music from then onwards. They combined to present a comic opera *The Knight of the Road* later known as *The Irish Girl*. I revised this work with Michael Casey some years ago and staged it as *Freeny!*

It was in 1891 also that French's first wife died, and, jobless, he finally turned to the stage as a means of livelihood, touring the country on his bicycle with a box of paints on his back. Eventually, at the age of fifty, he moved to London to widen his theatrical field, and although he always considered his artistic work as being the most important thing in in his life, worked at his stage career until in 1920 he died after a short illness at the home of a cousin in Formby, Lancashire, where he is buried.

Much of French's artistry died with him of course — a matter of voice, expression and timing — but the songs remain, and have become firmly entrenched in the folklore of Irish song. While humorous and ironic they never ridicule, and show a genuine love for the Irish country people about whom he wrote. It would be true to say that the songs of Percy French are more popular today than ever they have been.

They form an important section in my own one-man show and I have been pleased and surprised at how much they are appreciated in, for instance, the United States in places which never heard of Percy French before. It was for that reason that we decided to bring out this selection of the best known — and some of the lesser known — songs from my book *Percy French and his Songs*.

James N. Healy
1983

Contents

1. Abdulla Bulbul Ameer   **9**

Written in 1877, it is the earliest recorded song by Percy French. Composed for a 'smoking concert' while a student at Trinity, he sold it to an unscrupulous publisher for £5. Later it became very popular, and the names of others appeared as author, but French never drew a ha'penny in royalties. This is the original version.

2. Sweet Marie   **10**

Written as a 'take off' of a popular American tune, it nevertheless is redolent of French's youth in the west of Ireland, and like the song following breathes the spirit of the Irish 'Point-to-Point' races.

3. Rafferty's Racin' Mare   **12**

Another lively song about an Irish race-meeting.

4. The Hoodoo   **14**

The 'Nigger Minstrel' shows were enjoying a period of great popularity in French's early days. In his own district, and later with a troupe called 'The Kinniepottle Komics' in Cavan, he took part in the craze. This number was in later years used in a London show.

5. The Oklahoma Rose   **15**

Written in 1910, but also harking back to the 'Blackface' days. The banjo, associated with such troupes, was the instrument French used to accompany himself.

6. Phil the Fluther's Ball   **17**

A product of Cavan days: an early song and one of the liveliest and best. 'Phil' was a real character on the Leitrim-Sligo border who gave parties in his home in an attempt to pay the rent.

7. Come Back Paddy Reilly   **18**

Written in 1912, but really a memory of his days in Cavan. Paddy Reilly also was a real life person who had left his home town of Ballyjamesduff to go abroad. A splendid song in any context.

8. Shlathery's Mounted Fut   **20**

The idea of a national Irish Army emerging (as it did thirty years after this song was written in 1889) would have been thought unlikely, to say the least, in French's day, especially in the society to which he naturally belonged; but he himself was not political, and he shared a mutual respect with the country people about whom he wrote. So there was nothing derogatory in his mind when writing about 'Shlathery' — it is purely a comic song of great life and spirit.

9. Andy McElroe   **22**

While, as said, a national army was not envisaged at the time many Irishmen joined the existing British army and served abroad. Andy was one of several such in Percy's songs — a 'hero' out for divilment who was sure to strike terror into the heart of any foe. 'J. Ross' his collaborator was Sir John Ross. It was, in 1888, French's first song to be published after 'Abdulla Bulbul Ameer'.

10. Fighting McGuire   **24**

French obviously did not like bullies or windbags. McGuire is one such who is taught a lesson. The tune was lost until about twenty years ago when it was found in the British Museum.

11. The Girl on a Big Black Mare   26
An apparently straightforward love song tempered by the logic of the last few lines.

12. Mat Hannigan's Aunt   26
Written in 1892 for a topical review called *Dublin—Up-to-Date* which he performed with Richard Orpen, later an architect, and Orpen's younger brother William, who was to become famous as a painter, and be knighted.

13. Little Brigid Flynn   28
A charming number with a plaintive tune on one of French's favourite song themes — the prospective suitor sighing in a wryly-comic way about the bride he would like to have: effective because he never over-lapsed into sentiment — there was always a twinkle in the eye.

14. Mick's Hotel   29
One of the few occasions when French satirised in genuine anger — written after he had been overcharged for very poor service in an hotel while on his travels through Ireland. However, he would never reveal the name, or location, of the offending hostelry!

15. The Mountains of Mourne   31
Probably Percy French's most famous song. It has been sung, and parodied, thousands of times, but still retains its original charm. He wrote it one clear day in 1896 when the Mourne Mountains were visible on the horizon from the Hill of Howth, and sent the lyric to Collisson on the back of a postcard.

16. When Erin Wakes   33
The naïve side of Percy's nature. He saw nothing contradictory in writing this apparently patriotic song in 1900, and in the same year writing another welcoming King Edward to Ireland most effusively! It proved nothing except he loved Ireland and wished the country well on all counts.

17. McBreen's Heifer   34
Again one of the very best songs, with a typical Irish countryside situation. Should Jamesy take the good-looking daughter on her own, or take the ugly one with a heifer thrown in? In the end he took too long to make up his mind.

18. The Fortunes of Finnegan   35
Finnegan was one of those tough, enduring Irishmen for whom French showed cautious respect. The date of the song is uncertain, but it was written in collaboration with Collisson for one of their London concert seasons.

19. Mulligan's Masquerade   37
The song, of good-natured chaos at an Irish country party, may have been based on the memory of a real occasion: at any rate I have been to some like it! There are similar songs by other authors, such as 'The Tipperary Christening', 'McCarthy's Party', and even 'Lannigans Ball'.

20. The Night that Miss Cooney Eloped   39
Percy French first performed this number at a concert in the midlands, and was surprised when almost the entire front row walked out: but even more so at the hysterical laughter and cheers with which the rest of the audience greeted his efforts. What he did *not* know was that those who departed were the local Cooney family, big wigs in their own minds, who had lately endured an almost identical trauma to that described in the song. In fact he had never heard of them before, and had written about an imaginary situation.

21. Drumcolliher   41
Based on an older ballad called 'Kildorrery'. Drumcolliher is to the east, and Kildorrery about equidistant to the west, from Charleville.

22. Jim Wheelahan's Automobeel   43
'Automobiles', as motor cars were known in early days, were a new wonder in French's time, and regarded with some distrust. They were rare objects but were beginning to make their noisy presence heard on roads which had formerly been quiet byways. French seemed to mis-

trust things mechanical as will be seen in some of the later songs.

23. 'Are Ye Right There, Michael?'   45

Again one of the gems of Percy French songwriting, based on a genuine incident. The train carrying him from Ennis to Kilkee broke down and he was late for the concert. This was in 1897; French took an action for 'loss of profits', was awarded £10 and the company lost an appeal. The song came out in 1902 and although the company contemplated a libel action they wisely thought better of it. They had had enough.

24. Eileen Oge   46

Again, one of Percy's best songs on the locale nearest his heart — the countryside of his beloved west of Ireland. Ruefully and comically he presents the story of the disappointed suitor.

25. Donegan's Daughter   48

A first-class number which, strangely, is not heard as often as some of the others. Donegan's daughter from the 'States' is not as glamorous as at first appeared.

26. Father O'Callaghan   50

Collisson, a Protestant clergyman, had many friends among the Catholic priesthood and he asked French to write some verses so that he could set them to music as a tribute to one of his priest friends.

27. Maguire's Motor Bike   52

Again, we hear of French's mistrust of anything mechanical, particularly those noisy two-wheeled machines which continue to be a curse and potential danger on our roads today. The bike was all right in the end, but Maguire was buried beside it!

28. Phistlin' Phil McHugh   54

A charming number which, like 'Donegan's Daughter', is not as frequently heard as some of the others. Phil was a typical French rover who came home to roost in the end.

29. No More of Yer Golfin' for Me   55

French was no bad sportsman, but could never understand people being so anxious about winning. The fascination of golf was, however, a mystery to him.

30. The Darlin' Girl from Clare   57

The county of Clare was one of Percy's happiest hunting grounds and he performed at Kilkee whenever he could, using the occasion to make water-colours in the wonderfully clear air of the area. 'The Darlin' Girl' is a charming song. He made a ladies' version for his singing partner of later years, May Laffan.

31. Pretendy Land   59

Written in 1907 for *Noah's Ark*, a Christmas fairy play with music by J. A. Robertson. It reflects the love of children which French exhibited so strongly with his own family, and which has been reflected back to him by them through all the years since.

32. Mrs Brady   60

Composed for a London concert season, and which Collisson apparently sang well. One has a feeling, however, that some of these late songs, with music composed especially by Collisson, do not have the spontaneity of the earlier purely French numbers.

33. Flaherty's Drake   62

Based on the same idea as the much older ballad 'Ned, or Nell, Flaherty's Drake' but bearing no resemblance to it in construction.

34. The Mary Ann McHugh   63

Again based on the idea of an older ballad 'The Cruise of the Calabar' but the late Philip Green wrote new music to it in 1962. I have restored the original music which was partly the tune of 'Limerick is Beautiful' as this was French's original intention, and completed the rest of the tune myself.

35. The Kerry Courting
65

French wrote this lively little miniature operetta for four voices in 1909. I give the opening number about the 'Rose of Tralee'.

36. A Sailor Courted a Farmer's Daughter
66

Take off of the traditional Irish countryside singers come-all-ye style and very amusing.

37. Tullinahaw
68

One of the better neglected lyrics, although the music does not, perhaps, come up to the words. Probably written about 1910.

38. The Emigrant's Letter
69

In 1910 there was a great adventure for the two little men, French and Collisson — French was only five feet four inches and Collisson was shorter — when they set out on an American tour. The steamer called at Cobh where it took on the inevitable emigrants. As a fresh young fellow was saying goodbye to his relatives he said ruefully, 'They'll be cutting the corn in Creeshla the day.' It was autumn and the harvest was coming in.

39. Kitty Gallagher
72

In French's litany of love affairs the prize usually goes to the bold-hearted lover, as in 'Eileen Oge' and 'The Darlin' Girl from Clare'; however, Kitty chooses the man who gets knocked out for her sake.

40. Flanagan's Flying Machine
73

Written in 1911. It further demonstrates his mistrust of the mechanical — he preferred the open road and his bicycle. Nevertheless, by the last verse, he seems to accept the inevitability of the future.

41. 'Who said the Hook never hurted the Worms?'
75

42. I Fought a Fierce Hyena
76

Two numbers from *Freda and the Fairies*, a delightful miniature 'opera' suitable for children of junior school, with music by Caroline Maude (Viscountess Hawarden), and some of the lyrics by Cecily Fox-Smith. The first number seems to speak up against cruelty to animals, and the second to foreshadow by many years 'I can do anything' from *Annie Get Your Gun*.

43. The Killyran Wrackers
77

The tune of this number had been lost, but when writing *Percy French and His Songs* in the early sixties I got in touch with Vincent Sheils of Loughrea through my friend Michael Collins-Powell, and he was able to supply part of it from memory. In order to complete the number I have taken the liberty of finishing the tune in the same manner.

By 1914 the First World War had come, and French wrote several songs favouring the Allied side. French continued to entertain during war time, on one occasion right through a Zeppelin raid. When this passed off he commented calmly to the audience, 'Now wasn't that a nice Air Raid?'

44. Larry Mick McGarry
79

The last song Percy French wrote — in 1915. He gave the cook a ticket for the concert at which he was to sing it for the first time, and when she came home the family were naturally anxious to discover how things had gone. Her reply, as she went stamping downstairs, was 'He did that ou'l song he's been practisin' up there for the last days without end!'

During his last years French wrote no more, depending from then on the large repertory he had built up over the years. As has been said, he died in 1920 performing almost to the end. However, as long as his songs survive he will be remembered, and one hopes this little book will help him to be remembered for some time longer. You won't go too far wrong at a party with a Percy French song.

1. Abdulla Bulbul Ameer

As originally written and composed by Percy French

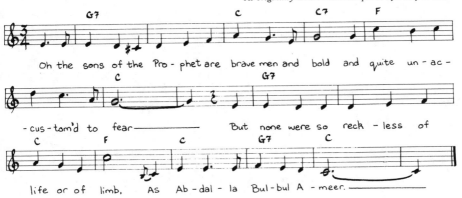

Oh the sons of the Pro-phet are brave men and bold and quite un-ac--cus-tom'd to fear—— But none were so reck-less of life or of limb, As Ab-dal-la Bul-bul A-meer.——

When they wanted a man to encourage the van
Or to harrass the foe in the rear
Or to take a redoubt they would always sent out
For Abdulla Bulbul Ameer.

There are heroes in plenty, and well known to fame
In the ranks that were lead by the Czar,
But the bravest of all was a man by the name
Of Ivan Potschjinksi* Skidar.
He could imitate Toole, play Euchre and Pool
And perform on the Spanish guitar.
In fact quite the cream of the Muscovite team
Was Ivan Potschjinski Skidar.

One morning the Russian had shouldered his gun
And assumed his most truculent sneer
And was walking down town when he happened to run
Into Abdulla Bulbul Ameer.
'Young man,' says Bulbul, 'can your life be so dull
That you're anxious to end your career? –
For, infidel, know – you have trod on the toe
Of Abdulla Bulbul Ameer.

Take your ultimate look upon sunshine and brook,
Make your latest remarks on the war;
Which I mean to imply that you're going to die,
Mr Count Cask-o-whisky Cigar.'
Said the Russian, 'My friend, my remarks in the end
Would avail you but little, I fear,
For you'll never survive to repeat them alive,
Mr Abdulla Bulbul Ameer.'

Then the bold Mameluke drew his trusty chiboque
And shouted, 'Il Allah Akbar.'

9

And being intent upon slaughter, he went
For Ivan Potschjinski Skidar.
But just as his knife had abstracted his life
(In fact he was shouting 'Huzza!')
He felt himself struck by that subtle Calmuck,
Count Ivan Potschjinski Skidar.

The Consul drove up in his red-crested fly
To give the survivor a cheer,
He arrived just in time to exchange a goodbye
With Abdulla Bulbul Ameer.
And Skobeleff, Gourko and Gorschekoff too
Drove up on the Emperor's car.
But all they could do was cry 'Och-whilliloo!'
With Ivan Potschjinski Skidar.

There's a grave where the waves of the Blue Danube roll
And on it in characters clear
Is: 'Stranger, remember to pray for the soul
Of Abdulla Bulbul Ameer.'
A Muscovite maiden her vigil doth keep
By the light of the true lover's star
And the name that she murmurs so sadly in sleep
Is Ivan Potschjinski Skidar.

* Pronounced like a sneeze.

2. Sweet Marie

Music based on old American Tune

hoult Sweet Ma-rie If you bolt Sweet Ma-rie Sure you'll nev-er win the farm-er's cup for me —— And if you don't pull it through, faith I'm done and so are you, For I'll trade you off for glue Sweet Ma-rie. ——

Now, the colours that I chose for Sweet Marie
Were Lavender and Rose for Sweet Marie,
Och, but now, no thanks to you, sure I'm quite another hue,
For I'm only black and blue, Sweet Marie.
    Hould your hoult, Sweet Marie,
    If you bolt, Sweet Marie,
    Sure, you'll never win the Farmer's Cup for me.
    Every daisy in the dell ought to know me mighty well,
    For on every one I fell, Sweet Marie.

Now we're started for the Cup, my Sweet Marie,
Weight for age and owners up, my Sweet Marie,
Owners up just now I own, but the way you're waltzing roun'
Sure, 'twill soon be owners down, Sweet Marie.
    Hould your hoult, Sweet Marie,
    Pass the colt, Sweet Marie,
    Och, you've gone and lost the Farmer's Cup for me,
    Your're a stayer too, I find: but you're not the proper kind
    For you stay too far behind, Sweet Marie.

3. Rafferty's Racin' Mare

Composed by Houston Collisson

You've not seen Raff-er-ty round this way? He's a man with a bro-ken hat His
tie and his col-lar are all gone a-stray, And his coat for the mat-ter o' that. We're
rac-in' Raff-er-ty round the place, Since Raff-er-ty raced his mare. He's a
man with an anx-ious look on his face, And a par-tial-ly murth-er'd air.
Oh—— Raff-er-ty's rac-in' mare We met him at the fair Says
he "She'll win, so keep yer tin for back-in' the rac-in' mare", Oh——
Raff-er-ty's rac-in' mare We thank'd him then and there And
ev-'ry lad in Bal-lin-a-fad, Went back-in' the rac-in' mare.

I was the jockey they chose to ride –
And often the owner he sware
That there wasn't a leap in the earth too wide
To baffle the racin' mare.
Over hurdle and ditch she went like a witch,
Till she came where the water shone –
I gave her her head, but she stopped at it dead:
She stopped – and I went on!

Chorus: Oh! Rafferty's racin' mare –
              I whirtled through the air
              Like a beautiful bird, but never a word
              From Rafferty's racin' mare!

'Get up, you lad,' says Ballinafad,
'You'll win the race for us yet.'
But I didn't care for the look of the mare,
Nor the way that her legs were set.
Says they: 'The horse'll stay the course,
She'll stay it – every foot.'
'You're right,' says I – 'I don't deny
She'll stay just where she's put.'

Chorus: Oh! Rafferty's racin' mare –
              We danced around her there.
              With stones and sticks, and bits o' bricks
              We hit her fair and square.
              Oh! Rafferty's racin' mare –
              The field they lept it there,
              But on the brink she'd stand and – drink,
              Would Rafferty's racin' mare.

But where was Rafferty all the time?
Oh! Rafferty! he's the lad,
There in the ring – he stood like a king,
Cheerin' the mare like mad,
His brother was there, disguised, of course,
As a Roosian millionaire;
Giving the odds against every horse
And the longest against the mare.

Chorus: Oh! Rafferty's racin' mare –
              'Twas more than we could bear,
              When a bookie revealed
              He was backin' the field,
              Instead of the racin' mare.
              We've got the day to spare,
              We've got the millionaire;
              And we're havin' a race around the place,
              And Rafferty – he's the hare!

4. The Hoodoo

Composed by Houston Collisson

When de stars be - gin to peep   and de moon am shin - in'
In - to our cab - in homes we creep   me and Lin-dy Loo.
Out of his cave dere comes de Hoo-doo Yes! dere comes de creep-y, crawl-y Hoo-doo,
An' if a chile ain't in his bed De Hoo -doo'll catch him sure.
Whis - per low   when twi -light shades are fall - ing
Pull de clo'   a - roun' de curl - y head
To and fro   I hear de Hoo - doo call - in'
'Are dere an - y   lit -tle *picc*-an-in-ies who am not in bed?'

Once der was a wicked little girl
Not like ma Lindy!
Flat-foot niggeress name o' Sal
Said, 'I don't suppose
Dat der is anything like de Hoodoo
Shouldn't run away from it like you do!'
Where has she gone dat naughty little girl?
Only de Hoodoo knows!

Whisper low!
When twilight shades are falling
Pull de clo' around de curly head
To and fro I hear de Hoodoo calling –
'Are dere any little piccaninies who am not in bed?'

Work at night for dose we lub –
Dat scares de Hoodoo!
Den him sings like a turtle dove cooin' all night long,
Now dat we're one dat's what we do do,
Guess it's what I see ma Lindy Loo do
Wish for de little one dat we've got
Singin' de whole night thro'.

Chorus:

So I know,
When twilight shades are falling
Comes the foe de piccaninies dread,
Soft and slow I hear de Hoodoo calling –
'Are dere any little piccaninies who am not in bed?'

5. The Oklahoma Rose

Composed by Percy French

All round de moon Clouds are hang-in' high an ha-zy; On de la-goon Moon-beams are ly-in' la-zy.

Dat's when dis coon's g'wine to meet ma Mai-sie, An' I'm sing-in' de same old song. It's

not a-bout ma Di-nah 'Way down in Ca-ro-li-na, Ma la-test love is fin-er Dan

an-y flow'r dat blows. In fact, she don't re-mind me Of gals I've left be-hind me, For

true loves chains dey bind me To Ok-la-ho-ma's rose. She can trip like

moon-beams on de wa-ter; Ev-'ry step dis col-our'd coon he taught her.

Just one clip a-round her waist I caught her When de band play'd "Mum-bling

Mose." She's ma rose, Ma li-ly an' ma dai-sy; Whar she goes de

col-our'd coons go cra-zy. All I knows is ma A-min-ta Mai-sie Am de

Ok-la-ho-ma rose. Ok-la-ho-ma rose.

All through de day she keeps lookin' down demurely,
    Much as to say – 'I can't be a woman surely!
I still can play with ma doll securely,
    For dis ain't de time to spoon.'
But when de sun am sinkin' her eyes begin a winkin'
An' den I know she's thinkin' of dis yer colour'd coon.
Oh! ain't I glad I found her. In love chains I have bound her.
    Her face is rather rounder — it's rounder dan de moon.

Chorus: She hears me call an' she comes a-creepin', creepin',
    Over de wall she sees me leapin', leapin',
Big folks an' small quietly are sleepin',
    When I meet ma lily belle.
Up an' down de ladder I'm slippin' like a shadder,
    No one could be gladder dan me, I don't suppose.
I'm coaxin' her an' teasin', I'm kissin' her an' squeezin',
    It seems to me it's pleasin' to Oklahoma's Rose.

16

6. Phil the Fluther's Ball

Composed by Percy French

There was Misther Denis Dogherty, who kep' the runnin' dog;
There was little crooked Paddy, from the Tiraloughett bog;
There was boys from every Barony, and girls from ev'ry 'art'
And the beautiful Miss Bradys, in a private ass an' cart,
And along with them came bouncing Mrs Cafferty,
Little Micky Mulligan was also to the fore,
Rose, Suzanne, and Margaret O'Rafferty,
The flower of Ardmagullion, and the pride of Pethravore.   *Chorus:*

First, little Micky Milligan got up to show them how,
And then the Widda' Cafferty steps out and makes her bow,
'I could dance you off your legs,' sez her, 'as sure as you are born,
If ye'll only make the piper play "The Hare was in the Corn".'
So Phil plays up to the best of his ability,
The lady and the gentleman begin to do their share;
'Faith then Mick, it's you that has agility:
Begorra Mrs Cafferty, yer leppin' like a hare!'   *Chorus:*

Then Phil the Fluther tipped a wink to little Crooked Pat,
'I think it's nearly time,' sez he, 'for passin' round the hat.'
So Paddy pass'd the caubeen round, and looking mighty cute
Sez, 'Ye've got to pay the piper when he toothers on the flute.'
Then all joined in wid the greatest joviality,
Covering the buckle, and the shuffle, and the cut;
Jigs were danced, of the very finest quality,
But the Widda' bet the company at 'handling the fut'.   *Chorus:*

7. Come Back Paddy Reilly

Written and composed by Percy French

18

green a - round Bal - ly - james - duff and the blue sky is ov - er it all ——— And tones that are ten - der, and tones that are gruff, are whis - per - ing ov - er the sea ——— Come back Pad - dy Reil - ly to Bal - ly - james - duff, Come home Pad - dy Reil - ly to me. ———

My mother once told me that when I was born,
The day that I first saw the light,
I looked down the street on that very first morn,
And gave a great crow of delight.
Now most new born babies appear in a huff,
And start with a sorrowful squall
But I knew I was born in Ballyjamesduff,
And that's why I smiled on them all.
The baby's a man, now he's toil-worn and tough,
Still, whispers come over the sea,
'Come back, Paddy Reilly, to Ballyjamesduff,
Come home, Paddy Reilly, to me.'

The night that we danced by the light of the moon,
Wid Phil to the fore with his flute.
When Phil threw his lip over 'Come again soon'
He'd dance the foot out o' yer boot!
The day that I took long Magee by the scruff,
For slanderin' Rosie Kilrain,
Then marchin' him straight out of Ballyjamesduff

19

Assisted him into a drain.
Oh, sweet are me dreams, as the dudeen I puff,
Of whisperings over the sea,
'Come back, Paddy Reilly, to Ballyjamesduff,
Come home, Paddy Reilly, to me.'

I've loved the young women of every land —
That always came easy to me,
Just barrin' the belles of the Black-a-moor brand,
And the chocolate shapes of Feegee.
But that sort of love is a moonshiny stuff,
And never will addle me brain.
For the bells will be ringin' in Ballyjamesduff,
For me and me Rosie Kilrain!
And all through their glamour, their gas, and their guff,
A whisper comes over the sea,
'Come back, Paddy Reilly, to Ballyjamesduff,
Come home, Paddy Reilly, to me.'

8. Shlathery's Mounted Fut

Written and composed by Percy French

You've heard of Jul-ius Cae-sar, and the great Nap-o-leon too
And how the Cork Mil-i-tia bate the Turks at Wat-er-loo.
But there's a page of glo-ry that as yet re-mains un-cut,
And that's the war-like sto-ry of the Shlath-er-y's Mount-ed Foot!
This gal-lant corps was or-gan-ised by Shlath-er-y's eld-est son
A no-ble mind-ed poach-er with a doub-le-breast-ed gun
And

20

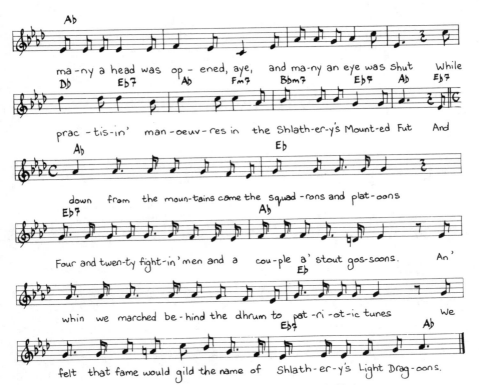

ma-ny a head was op - ened, aye, and ma-ny an eye was shut While

prac -tis-in' man -oeuv -res in the Shlath-er-y's Mount-ed Fut And

down from the moun-tains came the squad -rons and plat-oons

Four and twen-ty fight-in' men and a cou-ple a' stout gos-soons. An'

whin we marched be-hind the dhrum to pat -ri -ot-ic tunes We

felt that fame would gild the name of Shlath-er-y's Light Drag-oons.

Well, first we reconnoithered round O'Sullivan's Shebeen –
It used to be 'The Shop House', but we call it, 'The Canteen',
But there we saw a notice which the bravest heart unnerved –
'All liquor must be settled for before the dhrink is served.'
So on we marched, but soon again each warrior's heart grew pale,
For risin' high in front o' us we saw the County Jail;
And when the army faced about, 'twas just in time to find
A couple o' stout policemin had surrounded us behind.

Chorus: Still, from the mountains came the squadrons and platoons,
Four-an'-twinty fightin' min, an' a couple o' sthout gossoons;
Says Shlattery, 'We must circumvent these bludgeonin' bosthoons,
Or else it sames they'll take the names o' Shlathery's Light Dragoons.'

'We'll cross the ditch,' our leader cried, 'an' take the foe in flank.'
But yells of consthernation here arose from every rank,
For posted high upon a tree we very plainly saw,
'Threspassers prosecuted, in accordance wid' the law'.
'We're foiled!' exclaimed bould Shlathery, 'here ends our grand campaign,
'Tis merely throwin' life away to face that mearin' drain,
I'm not as bold as lions, but I'm braver nor a hin,
An' he that fights and runs away will live to fight agin.'

21

An' back to the mountains went the squadrons and platoons,
Four-an'-twinty fightin' min, an' a couple o' sthout gossoons;
The band was playing cautiously their patriotic tunes;
To sing the fame, if rather lame o' Shlattery's Light Dragoons.'

9. Andy McElroe

Written with Sir John Ross

My bro-ther An-dy said, that for a sol-dier he would go, So
great ex-cite-ment came up-on the house of Mc-El-Roe. My fa-ther sold a
bog-hole to e-quip him for the war, And my mo-ther sold the cush-ions of her
Sun-day jaunt-ing car, And when brave An-dy reach'd the front, 'Twas fur-ious work he
made, They ap-point-ed him a pri-vate in the Croc-o-dile Bri-gade. The
Sound of An-dy's bat-tle cry struck ter-ror thro' the foe, His
foot was on the des-ert and his name was Mc-El-Roe. At

Chorus

least that's what the let-ter said that came a-cross the foam, To

22

And-y's an-xious rel-a-tives a-wait-ing him at home. The pa-pers say he ran a-way be-fore he met the foe, But that was quite un-like the style of An-dy Mc-El-roe.

One morning brave Lord Wolseley for a battle felt inclined;
But all could see the general had something on his mind;
Sez he, 'My staff, 'twere dangerous to face yon deadly foe,
Unless we're sure that quite prepared is Andy McElroe.'
Then Andy cried, 'I'm here, my lord, and ready for the fray,'
'Advance then,' cried Lord Wolseley, 'and let every trumpet bray.'
Then England, Ireland, Scotland, rolled together on the foe,
But far ahead of everyone rushed Andy McElroe.

Chorus: At least, that's what the letter said that came across the foam
To Andy's anxious relatives, awaiting him at home.
The government despatches had another tale – but no!
We won't believe a word against brave Andy McElroe.

The Mahdi had gone up a tree, a spyglass in his eye,
To see his Paynim chivalry the northern prowess try;
But soon he saw a form of dread, and cried in tones of woe,
'Be jabers let me out of this – there's Andy McElroe.'
Then down he hurried from his tree, and straight away he ran,
To keep appointments, as he said, in distant Kordofan,
And fled those Arab soldiery like sand siroccos blow,
Pursued (with much profanity) by Andy McElroe.

Chorus: At least, that's what he told us when returning o'er the foam
To greet his anxious relatives, awaiting him at home.
So sing the song of triumph, and let all your bumpers flow,
In honour of our countryman, brave Andrew McElroe.

10. Fighting McGuire

Composed by Percy French

Oh, Gib-bon has told the sto-ry of old of the fall of the Rom-an Em-pire But I would re-call the rise an' the fall of a man by the name of Mc-Guire. He came to our town as a man of re-nown, and peace was, he said, his de-sire, Still he'd fre-quent-ly state what would be the sad fate, of the man who mo-les-ted Mc-Guire.

Well, we all were afraid of this quarrelsome blade,
An' we told him to draw near the fire,
An' laughed at his jest, tho' it wasn't the best,
An' swore there's no man like McGuire.
An' when he came up with the neighbours to sup,
His friendliness all would admire,
An' he'd have the best bed – for we'd sleep in the shed
For fear of insulting McGuire.

But MacGilligan's Dan – who's a rale fightin' man,
Said, 'Of all this tall talkin' I tire,
I'll step in an' see whyever should he
Be called always Fightin' McGuire.
I'll step in and say, in a casual way,
That I think he's a thief and a liar,
Then I'll hit him a clout, and unless I misdoubt,
That's a way of insulting McGuire.'

Then onward he strode to McGuire's abode,
His glorious eye shootin' fire,
And we thought as he passed we have all looked our last
On the man who insulted McGuire;
Then we listened with grief while we heard him called thief,
An' abused as a rogue an' a liar;
Oh, we all held our breath, for we knew it was death
To give any chat to McGuire.

Well, the row wasn't long, but 'twas hot an' 'twas strong
An' the noise it grew higher an' higher
Then it stopt! – an' we said, 'Oh begorra, he's dead!
He's been kilt out an' out by McGuire!'
Then out like a thrush from a hawthorn bush
Came something in tattered attire,
And after it fled the man we thought dead –
The man who malthreated McGuire.

'Twas MacGilligan's son, the victory won,
An' we crowded around to admire
The bowld-hearted boy who was first to destroy
The Yoke of the Tyrant McGuire.
An' altho' it's not true, we all said that we knew
From the first he was only a liar,
An' we'd all had a mind to attack – from behind –
That cowardly scoundrel – McGuire.

11. The Girl on a Big Black Mare

From 'The Irish Girl': original music by Houston Collisson
Re-written, as here, for 'Freeny' (1975) by Michael Casey

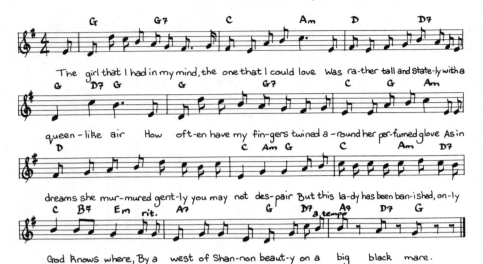

The girl that I had in my mind, the one that I could love Was ra-ther tall and state-ly with a queen-like air How oft-en have my fin-gers twined a-round her per-fumed glove As in dreams she mur-mured gent-ly you may not des-pair But this la-dy has been ban-ished, on-ly God knows where, By a west of Shan-non beaut-y on a big black mare.

I dreamt of floating idly on a gentle flowing stream,
    A siren seated by me with her golden hair,
Who sang to me sweet melodies that echoed through my dream,
    And while the vision lasted all the earth was fair.
But now my nightly vision and my daily care
Is the girl who nearly brained me with her big black mare.

12. Mat Hannigan's Aunt

Composed by Percy French

Oh! Mat Han-ni-gan had an Aunt An Un-cle too like-wise; But in this chant, 'tis Han-ni-gan's Aunt I wish to eu-lo-gise. For when young lov-ers came And axed her to be theirs, Mat

26

Han-ni-gan's Aunt took each gal-lant And fir'd him down the stairs, And fir'd him down the stairs. So here's a health to Han-ni-gan's Aunt, I'll tell you the rea-son why She al-ways had things da-cent in the Han-ni-gan fam-i-ly A plat-ther an' can for ev-'ry man, "What more did the qual-i-ty want? You've yer bite an' yer sup, what's cock-in' yees up!" says Mat-hew Han-ni-gan's Aunt.

Oh! she never would raise her voice,
    She never was known to scold,
But when Hannigan' Aunt sed, 'No, you can't,'
    You did what you were told;
And if anyone answered back,
    Oh, then his hair she'd comb.
'For all I want,' sez Hannigan's Aunt,
    'Is peace in our happy home.'

Chorus: So here's a health. . .

Oh, when she went to Court,
    The A-de-congs in vain
Would fume and rant, for Hannigan's Aunt
    Said, 'Boy, let go me thrain!'
And when the Lard Leftinant
    A kiss on her brow would imprint!
'Oh no, you can't' said Hannigan's Aunt
    'Widout me pa's consint.'

Chorus: So here's a health. . .

27

Oh, 'tis often we'd praise her up,
  We'd laud her to the sky,
We'd all descant on Hannigan's Aunt
  And hope she never would die.
But still I'd like to add –
  If Hannigan isn't about –
That whin we plant Mat Hannigan's Aunt,
  We won't be too put out.

Chorus: So here's a health. . .

13. Little Brigid Flynn

Composed by Percy French

I've a nice slat-ed house, and a cow or two at grass; I've a plant gar-den run-ning by the door; I've a shel-ter for the hens and a sta-ble for the ass, And what does a man want more. I dun-no, may-be so, And a bach-el-or is ais-y and he's free, But I've lots to look af-ter And I'm liv-ing all a-lone, And there's no-one look-ing af-ter me.

Me father often tells me I should go and have a try
To get a girl that owns a bit of land;
I know the way he says it there is someone in his eye,
And me mother has the whole thing planned.
I dunno, maybe so,
And 'twould molify them greatly to agree,
But there's Little Brigid Flynn,
Sure its her I'd like to win,
Though she never throws an eye at me.

28

Oh, there's a little girl who is worth her weight in gold,
An' that's a dacent dowry don't you see;
And I mean to go and ax her as soon as I get bold,
If she'll come and have an eye to me.
I dunno – will she go,
But I'd like to have her sittin' on me knee
And I'd sing like a thrush,
On a hawthorn bush
If she'll come and have an eye to me.

14. Mick's Hotel

Written and composed by Percy French

Has an-y-bo-dy ev-er been to Mick's Ho-tel, Mick's Ho-tel by the salt say wa-ter?

None o' yez ha' been there just as well! Just as well for ye! oh!

If ye were an os-the-ridge ye might con-trive To get a-way from the place a-live, They

charge you a dol-lar for a meal you could-n't swal-ler, And it's down by the sil-ver sea.

Oh yes I've been there Yes I was green there Hop-ing that the wait-er might per-

-haps at-tend to me   'What's in that tur-een there?' 'Soup sir, it's been there'

Nev-er a-gain for me.

I went up to the bedroom, but I couldn't find the soap.
'Soap! is it soap by the salt say water?'
I went to ring the bell, but I couldn't find the rope,
And the waiter says to me,
'What the divil do ye want with a bedroom bell,
Haven't you a voice, and can't you yell!'
I made the waiter holler! but it cost me a dollar
Down by the silver sea.
Oh yes, I've been there,
Wits sure are keen there,
But I was in no humour for the lad's jocosity;
Yes, I have been there,
Mick's King and Queen there.
Never again for me.

'You're waiting for your breakfast, sir, and now what will you take?
Fish! is it fish by the salt say water?
All gone up to Dublin, sir, before you were awake?'
'Kidneys and toast and tea.'
Well now, there was a kidney, but I think it was last week,
Oh, the tea and the toast isn't far to seek,
And marmalade to folla' that'll cost another dollar,
Down by the silver sea.
Oh yes, I've been there,
Hoping against hope for that second cup of tea.
Oh, yes, I've been there,
Shall I be seen there?
Never again for me.

'You're going in the morning, and you'll want to pay your bill.'
Bill! Oh, the bill by the salt say water!
If you want to see the size of it you've got to climb a hill,
Or spread it on the silver sea.
They work by 'double entry' – then they multiply by three
And still there's three and sixpence that they haven't got from me.
'Oh, ye washed his flannel collar, put down "Laundry–one dollar!"
Though you washed it in the silver sea.'
Oh yes, I've been there,
Cleaned out quite clean there.
The waiter can't explain the bill, and Mick you never see.
Oh, yes, I've been there,
I got quite lean there,
Never again for me.

15. The Mountains of Mourne

Arranged by Houston Collisson on traditional tune

Oh, Ma-ry this Lon-don's a won-der-ful sight, Wid the peo-ple here work-in' by day and by night: They don't sow pot-a-toes, nor bar-ley, nor wheat, But there's gangs o' them dig-gin' for gold in the street. At least, when I axed them that's what I was told, So I just took a hand at this dig-gin' for gold, But for all that I found there I might as well be Where the Moun-tains of Mourne sweep down to the sea.

I believe that, when writin', a wish you expressed
As to how the fine ladies in London were dressed.
Well, if you'll believe me, when axed to a ball,
They don't wear a top to their dresses at all!
Oh, I've seen them meself, and you could not, in thrath,
Say, if they were bound for a ball or a bath –
Don't be startin' them fashions now, Mary Machree,
Where the Mountains o' Mourne sweep down to the sea.

I seen England's king from the top of a 'bus –
I never knew him, though he means to know us:
And though by the Saxon we once were oppressed,
Still, I cheered – God forgive me – I cheered wid the rest.
And now that he's visited Erin's green shore,
We'll be much better friends than we've been heretofore
When we've got all we want, we're quiet as can be
Where the Mountains o' Mourne sweep down to the sea.

You remember young Peter O'Loughlin, of course –
Well, here he is now at the head o' the Force,
I met him today, I was crossing the Strand,
And he stopped the whole street wid wan wave of his hand.
And there we stood talking of days that are gone
While the whole population of London looked on;
But for all these great powers, he's wishful like me,
To be back where dark Mourne sweeps down to the sea.

There's beautiful girls here – oh, never mind! –
With beautiful shapes Nature never designed,
And lovely complexions, all roses and crame
But O'Loughlin remarked wid regard to them same:
'That if at those roses you venture to sip,
The colour might all come away on your lip.'
So I'll wait for the wild rose that's waitin' for me –
Where the Mountains o' Mourne sweep down to the sea.

16. When Erin Wakes

Air: 'The Flight of the Earls'

With spirit

Let new-er na - tions fill the stage And vaunt them to the sky, The
Gael has still a her - i -tage That gold can nev - er buy. The
moun -tains may be bleak and bare, For -lorn the coun-try - side But
as of old our head-lands bold Still front the rag -ing sea, So
great Cu - chul -ainn bat -tled there and Red Branch he - roes died. And
may our band u - nit - ed stand As fear - less and as free.

I hear the lays of other days
In martial numbers flow,
King Death's the only sword that stays
The march of Owen Roe.
At Fontenoy the breezes bore
The war cry of the Gael,
And Saxon standards fled before
The sons of Innisfail.
And as of old our headlands bold
Still front the raging sea,
So may our band united stand
As fearless and as free.

Beneath the rath the heroes sleep,
Their steeds beside them stand.
Each falchion from its sheath shall leap
To guard old Ireland:
The legend we may yet fulfil
And play the heroes part,
For Sarsfield's spirit slumbers still
In many an Irish heart;
And as of old our headlands bold
Still front the raging sea,
So may our band united stand
As fearless and as free.

17. McBreen's Heifer

Arranged and composed by Percy French

Mc Breen had two daugh-ters and each one in turn Was of-fered in mar-riage to Jam-esy O' Byrne Now kit-ty was pret-ty but Jane she was plain So to make up the dif-fer mc Breen would ex- plain He'd give the best hei-fer he had on the land As a sort of a bo - nus with Jane un-der-stand But then kit - ty would char-rum a bird off a bush And that left the lad in a hor- rid non - plush

Chorus

Now there's no de-ny-in' kit-ty was re-mark-a-b-ly pret-ty, Tho' I can't say the same for Jane, But still there's not the dif-fer of the price of a hei - fer, Be - tween the pret-ty and the plain.

Entirely bother'd was Jamesy O'Byrne
He thought that he'd give the school-master a turn;
Sez he, 'To wed Kitty is very good fun,
Still a heifer's a heifer when all's said an' done.
A girl she might lose her good looks anyhow –
And a heifer might grow to an elegant cow;
But still there's no price for the stock, d'ye mind.
And Jane has a face that the Divil designed.'

Chorus:

Now there's no denyin' Kitty was remarkably pretty,
Tho' I can't say the same for Jane,
But still there's not the differ of a the price of a heifer,
Between the pretty and the plain.

The school-master said, with a good deal of since,
'We'll reduce the two girls to shillin's an' pence,
Add the price of the heifer when Jane I'll be bound
Will come out the top by a couple o' pound.
But still I'm forgettin' that down in Glengall
The stock is just goin' for nothin' at all;'
So Jim thought he'd wait till the end of the year,
Till girls might be cheaper or stock might be dear.

Chorus:

But when he came for Kitty, she was married to McVittie,
And McBlane had appropriated Jane,
So whether there's the differ of the price of a heifer,
Is a thing that he never could explain.

18. The Fortunes of Finnegan

Music by Houston Collisson

'Twas Bran-a-gan an' Flan-a-gan Were talk-ing at the 'crass' When up comes Lar-ry Lan-a-gan A-driv-in' of an ass. Says he, "Poor Pet-er Fin-ne-gan Is laid out migh-ty flat — while rea-dy-in' his sup-per He was bit-ten by the cat". Says Bran-a-gan to Flan-a-gan, An' Flan-a-gan to Lan-a-gan, 'Lit-tle Pet-er Fin-ne-gan will not get ov-er that.' But lit-tle Pet-er Fin-ne-gan Is run-nin' out an' in a-gin', For

that wan taste of Fin-ne-gan Had par-a-lys'd the cat.

When Peter grew up big an' brown, a blacksmith he was made,
An' not a man in all the town could beat him at his trade,
One day to chase some corner boys he rushed out of his shed,
A motor-car was passin' an' it struck him on the head.

Chorus: Says Branagan to Flanagan, an' Flanagan to Lanagan,
'I hear that Peter Finnegan has gone to glory clean.'
But brawny Peter Finnegan's a horrid man to rin agin –
They found that Peter Finnegan was mendin' the machine.

The boys in all the Barony were courtin' Mary Flynn,
An' no one but that Finnegan would have a chance to win
All the others when they'd meet her 'bout the dowry would begin;
'But I'll take you, girl,' says Peter, 'in the clothes you're standin' in!'

Chorus: Says Branagan to Flanagan, an' Flanagan to Lanagan,
'It isn't Peter Finnegan she'll honour an' obey.'
But sorra a man but Finnegan will flirt wid Mary Flynn agin,
For bruisin' Peter Finnegan she married yesterday.

'Twas politics that Finnegan would study day an' night;
He'd argue right was mostly wrong an' black was really white,
And when the next election came the posters on the wall
Read, 'Vote for Peter Finnegan and the divil a tax at all!'

Chorus: Says Branagan to Flanagan, an' Flanagan to Lanagan,
'The vote that Peter votes himself his only vote will be.'
But Finnegan can win agin, no matter who he's in agin,
And bruisin' Peter Finnegan is Finnegan M.P.*

* Nowadays 'T.D.'

19. Mulligan's Masquerade

Written and composed by Percy French

Oh, the Mul-li-gans were the cham-pions at The High So-cie-ty game. Mol-ly

Mul-li-gan's danc-ing of the Paw de Cat, was an af-ter sup-per drame; Their

Fate Cham-pate was an il-li-gant trate, And so we all a-grade, If we

got an in-vi-ta-tion, we would not be late, At the Mul-li-gan's mas-quer-

ade. And Ger-ah-ty went as a 'Gon-do-lier', Pro-pel-ling an

ass and cart; Fo-gar-ty filled us

all wid fear as 'Na-po-lean Bo-na-parte.' The sup-per was great, all one could ate, On the

kitch-en dress-er laid; 'kitch-en dress-er' you say? We

Said 'Boo-fay' At Mul-li-gan's mas-quer-ade.

Bedalia Crow was 'Beautiful Snow'
And it made a curious blend;
O'Hooligan wasn't invited, so
He came as an 'Absent Friend'.
That boy of Magee's was 'Mefishtofeles',
But we called a spade a spade,
And not bein' civil, we called him 'The Divil'
At Mulligan's masquerade.

Chorus:

And Hennissy came as a 'Highwayman'
In the hat that his father wore,
They say that's the way that the father begun,
Amaxsin' his little store.
Miss Fay was seen as a Fairy Queen,
In a gauzy skirt arrayed;
We had to keep her behind the screen
At Mulligan's masquerade.

Miss Foxey Farrell was the 'Queen of France'
And the sight I shall never forget,
When Hogan, as Hamlet, begged a dance,
From 'Maryanne Toinette'.
Mrs Regan came as a 'Woodland Elf'
I don't know what she weighed,
But her very first prance broke all the delft
At Mulligan's masquerade.

Chorus:

Miss Casey, as 'Cycling', took the floor,
In corderoys and a kilt,
Her father patched up the old cuttamore
And came as a 'Crazy Quilt'.
Miss Mullaby as 'Joan of Cork'
Her beautiful shape displayed,
Faith! many a scarecrow you'd remark
At Mulligan's masquerade.

20. The Night that Miss Cooney Eloped

Written and composed by Percy French

Oh, boys, have ye heard o' them Coon-eys? Their ways would have filled ye with dread; They would — 'nt leave cards on the Roon-eys, An' cut Pat-sy Gal-la-gher dead. They ev — en looked down on the po-lis, An' held a mil-i-tia-man cheap: So the fam-i-ly felt that their pride got a welt When Miss Coon-ey e-loped with a sweep.

Ould Coon-ey was tear-in' his hair, An' said he'd not stay in the place; Mrs. Coon-ey she lepp'd off her chair, An' said, 'Twas a dy-in' dis-grace!' Young Coon-ey said he did-n't care, But he sat in the cor-ner an' moped. There was t'un-der and turf in the air, ye may swear, on the night that Miss Coon-ey e-loped.

Says Cooney, 'She's none o' me daughter,
And I won't have a sweep for me son;
If I meet them on land or water,
I'll knock their two heads into one.'
Says the son, 'Though he's famed as a fighter,
His death I will surely effect!'
But in this compact they lost sight of the fact
That the sweep would be sure to object.   *Chorus:*

Now the sweep was a terror to rassle.
And as to his fightin' – oh, there!
He always was king o' the castle,
At weddin' or wakin', or fair,
But, of course, wid the creme-de-la-cramers
He socially wasn't in touch –
As a sweep he would go to their houses, you know,
But was only admitted as such.   *Chorus:*

While they were abusin' the vill'in,
An' the daughter, through thick an' through thin,
An' swearin' she'd not have a shillin' –
The bride an' the bridegroom stepped in.
An' he lifted his fist up and shook it,
'I've married your daughter,' he said,
'So hand out the dower – and if ye look sour,
Be gomis! I'll have ye for dead!'

Chorus: So ould Cooney cried out, 'Lave it there,
All we want is contentment an' peace.'
Mrs Cooney sat down on her chair,
An' says she, 'You've an illigant face!'
Young Cooney said he didn't care,
It was better by far than he'd hoped.
Oh! the stream of goodwill it would turn a mill
On the night that Miss Cooney eloped!

21. Drumcolliher

Written and composed by Percy French

Moderato

I've been to a great ma-ny pla-ces And won-der-ful sights I've seen, From
Ag-her-na-voe to Bal-lin-a-sloe, And back by Bal-ly-por-een.
But when they talk of the towns that O-ver the o-cean lie When they
Say to me, 'Pat, what do you think of that?' I ups and I says, says I
I sup-pose you've not been to Drum-col-li-her? Ye haven't? Well, now I de-clare, You must
wait till you've been to Drum-col-li-her, And seen the fine place we have there. There's
on-ly one street in Drum-col-li-her, But then 'tis a glo-ry to see; Ye may
talk till you're dumb, but give me ould Drum, For Drum is the place for me.

41

They tell me there's Isles of the Ocean
By India's golden shore,
Where life all day long is a beautiful song,
With flowers and fruits galore;
They tell me the sun does be shining,
With never a cloud in the sky –
But when they have done with their clouds and their sun,
I ups and I says, says I –

Chorus: 'I suppose you've not been to Drumcolliher?
Ye haven't? Well now I declare,
You must wait till you've been to Drumcolliher,
And seen the fine sun we have there.
There's only one sun in Drumcolliher,
And then 'tis a glory to see;
You may talk till you're dumb, but give me ould Drum,
For Drum is the place for me.'

I was over in London quite lately,
I gave King Edward a call;
Says the butler, 'He's out, he isn't about,
An' I don't see his hat in the hall;
But if you like to look round, sir,
I think you will have to say,
Apartments like these are not what one sees
In your country every day.'

Chorus: Says I, 'Have yez been to Drumcolliher?
Ye haven't? Well now I declare,
You must wait till you've been to Drumcolliher,
And seen the fine house we have there.
There's only one house in Drumcolliher,
For hardware, bacon, and tea;
If your master would come we would treat him in Drum,
Oh! Drum is the place for me.'

22. Jim Wheelahan's Automobeel

Music by Houston Collisson

When Jim Wheel-a-han made all his mon-ey in trade, He said he'd as-ton-ish the town ——— And he stuck to his word, as you'll say when you've heard of the won-der-ful yoke he brought down ——— 'Twas the lat-est de-sign in the mot-or car line, Par-is-ien and ve-ry gen-teel ——— A mot-or might do for me or for you, But this was an aut-o-mo-beel. ———

Chorus

Jim Wheel-a-han's Aut-o-mo-beel, ——— oh that was the tath-er-in Wheel, ——— He tel-e-graph'd down he would ride thro' the town Next day in his aut-o-mo-beel. ———

He steered her until
He came nigh the long hill,
And he smiled as he rolled her along;
But the smile it gave way
To a look of dismay
When he found that the brake had gone
His father came out   [wrong,
To give him a shout:
Jim met him half-ways down the hill
And the last thing he said
As they put him to bed
Was. 'Hould on till I alther me will.'

Chorus:
Oh! Wheelahan's Automobeel!
It knocked the man head over heel;
It was only wan touch,
But he walks with a crutch
Since he met with the Automobeel!

We'd the band on a stand
And the town all on hand,
But they fled when he entered the square –
The beautiful stand
And the Emmett Brass Band
Was knocked to the divil knows where!
Blind 'Danny the Duck'
Had the worst bit of luck,
For the dog in the string it got furled;
And they found him full stritch
On his back in the ditch,
Lamentin' the end of the world!

Chorus:
When they said 'twas the Automobeel,
As they carried him home in a creel,
Says he, with a curse,
'I wish 'twas a hearse
Instead of his Automobeel!'

Now I'd have you note
That the quarryman's goat
Had been unwell that same night,
So for breakfast that day
She had just put away
A canful of strong dynamite.
Having taken her load,
She lay down on the road –
Even goats must digest such a meal –
And she didn't observe
Comin' sharp round the curve
Jim Wheelahan's Automobeel!

Chorus:
A bump! An explosion! A squeal –
We buried his hat and one wheel,
He's at rest – so are we,
For the country is free
From Wheelahan's Automobeel!

Encore Verse:
Jim Wheelahan's ghost
Took a run round the coast
On the day of the motor-car race,
And the wind bein' fair,
He was 'whooshed' thro' the air
At a rate even Edge daren't face.
When the winner came up
To receive the great cup,
His anger he could not conceal,
For there at the post
Was Jim Wheelahan's ghost,
Wid three-fourths of his Automobeel!

Chorus:
Says Edge, 'Be the laws, I'll appeal!
Such a record could never be real!'
Here the cock gave a crow,
And Jim vanished below,
With the ghost of his Automobeel!

23. 'Are Ye Right There, Michael?'

Written and composed by Percy French

You may talk of Col-um-bus-'s sail-ing A-cross the At-lan-tic-al Sea But he nev-er tried to go rail-ing From En-nis as far as Kil-kee You run for the train in the morn-ing, The ex-cur-sion train start-ing at eight You're there when the clock gives the warn-in', And there for an hour you'll wait And as you're wait-ing in the train, You'll hear the guard sing this re-frain— 'Are ye right there, Mi-chael, are ye right? Do you think that we'll be there be-fore the night? Ye've been so long in start-in', That ye could-n't say for sar-tin - Still ye might now, Mi-chael, so ye might!'

They find out where the engine's been hiding,
    And it drags you to Sweet Corofin;
Says the guard, 'Back her down on the siding
    There's the goods from Kilrush comin' in.'
Perhaps it comes in in two hours,
    Perhaps it breaks down on the way;
'If it does,' says the guard, 'be the powers
    We're here for the rest of the day!'

Spoken: And while you sit and curse your luck,
The train backs down into a truck.

'Are ye right there, Michael? Are ye right?
Have ye got the parcel there for Mrs White?
 Ye haven't, oh, begorra,
 Say it's comin' down tomorra –
And it might now, Michael, so it might.'

At Lahinch the sea shines like a jewel,
 With joy you are ready to shout,
When the stoker cries out, 'There's no fuel,
 And the fire's taytotally out.
But hand up that bit of log there –
 I'll soon have ye out of the fix;
There's a fine clamp of turf in the bog there.'
And the rest go a-gatherin' sticks.

Spoken: And while you're breakin' bits of trees,
You hear some wise remarks like these –

'Are ye right there, Michael? Are ye right?
Do ye think that you can get the fire to light?
 Oh, an hour you'll require,
 For the turf it might be drier –
Well, it might now, Michael, so it might.'

24. Eileen Oge

Arrangement by Houston Collisson

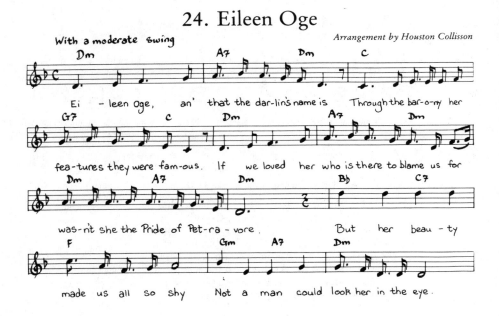

Boys o boys! sure that's the rea-son why we're in mourn-in' for the Pride of Pet-ra-vore. Ei-leen Oge! me heart is grow-in' grey Ev-er since the day you wan-dered far a-way Ei-leen Oge! there's good fish in the say, But there's no-one like the Pride of Pet-ra-vore.

Friday at the Fair of Ballintubber,
Eileen met McGrath, the cattle jobber,
I'd like to set me mark upon the robber,
For he stole away the Pride of Petravore.
He never seem'd to see the girl at all,
Even when she ogle'd him underneath her shawl,
Lookin' big and masterful, when she was looking small,
Most provokin' for the Pride of Petravore.   *Chorus*

So it went as it was in the beginning,
Eileen Oge was bent upon the winning,
Big McGrath contentedly was grinning,
Being courted by the Pride of Petravore.
Sez he, 'I know a girl that could knock you into fits,'
At that Eileen nearly lost her wits.
The upshot of the ruction was that now the robber sits,
With his arm around the Pride of Petravore.   *Chorus*

Boys, oh boys! with fate 'tis hard to grapple,
Of my eye 'tis Eileen was the apple.
And now to see her walkin' to the chapel
Wid the hardest featured man in Petravore.
And now, me boys, this is all I have to say,
When you do your courtin' make no display,
If you want them to run after you just walk the other way,
For they're mostly like the Pride of Petravore.   *Chorus*

25. Donegan's Daughter

Music by W. H. Collisson

When Don-e-gan came from the States Him-self and his daugh-ter were seen Pa-
-ra-ding the prin-ci-pal streets Of beaut-i-ful Bal-ly-po-reen Her
cheeks were as red as the rose Her hair was a beaut-i-ful brown And the
lads I sup-pose were as thick now as crows All tied to the heel of her gown. There were
short men and long men and weak men and strong men and right men and wrong men were
all to be seen But Don-e-gan's daugh-ter from ov-er the wa-ter She
gave them no quart-er in Bal-ly-po-reen.

She sang the most beautiful songs —
Of the words we had never a hint,
For her fingers went hammer and tongs
In a running accompaniment.
Like a dog running after a rat,
Such scrimmaging never was heard.
Then down went her claws, like a murdering cat
When it leps on the back of a bird.

Chorus:

At every party
She sang them all forte
From *Ah Che La Morte*
to *Wearin' the Green.*
Oh! Donegan's daughter,
From over the water,
'Twas little they taught her
In Ballyporeen.

The Geraghtys gave a grand ball,
The girls were all ribbons and tape
But Miss Donegan bested them all
With her perfectly wonderful shape;
And when she was taking the floor
With a high-stepping bachelor boy,
The rest of us scowled
In the doorway and growled
That 'twas him we would surely destroy.

Chorus:

There was kissing and squeezing
And coaxing and teasing
And sure there's no reason
Such things should be seen.
But Donegan's daughter
From over the water,
'Twas she made the slaughter
In Ballyporeen.

Coming home we were crossing a stream:
I thought to beleaguer the belle;
A struggle, a kiss, and a scream
And into the water we fell.
To me that can swim like a trout
It was only a trifling reverse:
But when she came out,
'Faith, there wasn't much doubt
She was changed very much for the worse.

Chorus:

For her roses had wilted,
Her wig it was tilted,
The figure she'd built, it
Was washed away clean:
Oh! Donegan's daughter
From under the water,
Two pins would have bought her
In Ballyporeen.

26. Father O'Callaghan

Music by Houston Collisson

Fa-ther Cor-nel-ius o' Call-a-ghan to most of us Fa-ther Con To

all of us quite the kind-li-est man that ev-er the sun shone on I

mind me when I was a bit of a lad He stood with me out in the cold While I

told him a cur-i-ous dream I'd had of find-in' a crock of gold

O Fa-ther O' Call - a -ghan When will the dream come true

O Fa-ther O' Call - a -ghan if an-y-one knows 'tis you And

Fa-ther O' Call-a-ghan strok'd me pate, sez he 'The sto-ry is old

Ev-e-ry man that can work and wait will find his crock of gold.'

Rosie Mulvany was bright as a bird,
　　I lov'd her, she didn't object,
But somehow I never could bring out the word,
　　That Rose had a right to expect.
I'd dream of her nightly, I'd dream she said, 'Yes.'
　　Be daylight me courage was gone,
I was wore to a shadow, so in my distress,
　　I went and I saw Father Con.

'O Father O'Callaghan,
    Will the dream come true?
O Father O'Callaghan,
    What is a boy to do?'
And Father O'Callaghan said, 'See here,
    You must call in your Sunday clothes,
Say to her this, "Will you marry me, dear?"
    You can leave the rest to Rose.'

We talk'd one night of the glorious days,
    When Ireland led the van,
With scholars as thick as the stars in the sky
    And work for every man.
''Twill come again,' said Father Con,
    And his fertile fancy paints
The glorious day when the sun shines on
    A new Isle of the Saints.

'O Father O'Callaghan,
    When will the dream come true?
O Father O'Callaghan,
    If anyone knows, 'tis you!'
And Father O'Callaghan raised his head,
    And smil'd his humoursome smile,
'When ev'ry man learns to rule himself
    'Twill then be a saintly Isle.'

Father O'Callagan's dead and gone,
    This many and many a day –
But we haven't forgot you, Father Con,
    And it keeps us from goin' astray.
And so at the last great earthquake shock,
    When the trumpet's soundin' clear,
He'll guide to their God the faithful flock,
    That knew him and lov'd him here.

'O Father O'Callaghan,
    When will the dream come true?
O Father O'Callaghan,
    If anyone knows 'tis you!'
And Father O'Callaghan says no word,
    For he's sleepin' softly yet,
And when the Archangel's voice is heard,
    We know that he won't forget.

27. Maguire's Motor Bike
(A Tragedy in Four Acts)

Music by Houston Collisson

It was Mick Ma-gui-re made it all a-lone and all un-aid-ed, For I
tell you that a brain-y boy was Mick, And for div-il-ment and murdh-er, Faith you
need-n't go no fur-ther than the bi-cy-cle he called the 'kill-me-quick'. Oh the
gear-case was a ket-tle made of good Brit-an-nia met-al As
good as you would buy in an-y shop, And when once you had it go-in', Faith there
nev-er was no know-in' where Ma-gui-re's mot-or bi-cy-cle would stop. But the
bike's all right, Not a bit it mat-tered, For the bike's all right And
none the worse for wear. Oh! the bike's all right – The
rid-er might be shat-tered, but the bike's all right, So Ma-gui-re does-n't care.

52

'Twould come whizzin' round a corner
And before you'd time to warn her
'Twould be through some poor old
       woman like a knife,
And Flynn the undertaker,
Said to Mike (that was the maker),
That he never was so busy in his life.
He'd lind it to relations
From whom he'd expectations,
And to folks for whom he didn't care.
Then Mick would say with sorrow,
'There'll be funerals tomorrow.'
And it somehow always happen'd that
       there were.

Chorus:
But the bike's all right,
His uncle tried to cycle,
Oh! the bike's all right,
And none the worse for wear.
The bike's all right,
The money went to Michael!
Oh! the bike's all right
So Maguire doesn't care.

They tried him for manslaughter,
But the case would not hold water,
For Maguire proved an alibi each time,
And not a one could shake him,
And divil a one could make him
In any ways accessory to crime.
They were gettin' quite alarmed,
And so a plot was formed,
A conspiracy they thought would never
       fail.
So they sought the level crossin'
When the 'nine o'clock' was passin'
And they laid it gintly down upon the rail.

Chorus:
Oh! the bike's all right,
Not a bit it mattered.
Oh! the bike's all right,
And none the worse for wear.
The bike's all right,
The nine o'clock was scatter'd,
But the bike's all right
So Maguire doesn't care.

Oh! the town was in a fury,
For at the next grand jury,
They were fined for an attempt to wreck the train
And out of the entire lot
'Twas only Mick Maguire got
Away from out the court without a stain.
So they held a monster meetin'
For the purpose of debatin'
A way to put the cycle on the shelf,
So at last it was decided,
And assinted, and provided,
That Maguire takes a ride on it himself.

Chorus:
The bike's all right,
Maguire tried to ride it,
Oh! the bike's all right,
Just as it was before.
The bike's all right,
They buried it beside him.
The bike's all right
But Maguire he's no more.

28. Phistlin' Phil McHugh

Written and composed by Percy French

There's Thady of the Cows —
Sure you know 'Ten-acre Thady',
With his fine new slated house,
He'd make her quite the lady,
But Thady needn't stay,
For there's no use his inthragin'
For her heart is far away —
'Tis wid Phil McHugh stravagin'. *Chorus:*

'Tis wisdom's golden rule
I do teach her till I tire,
That every girl's a fool,
Ay, and every man's a liar.
What's that, you say, you hear,
That's set you all a thrimbly,
'Tis but the wind I fear
That is phistlin' down the chimbly. *Chorus:*

There's Danny Michael Dan,
Who is six fut in his stockin's
A very proper man,
But she never heeds his knockin's
She'd keep him standin' there
For three-quarters of a minit,
But she's racin' like a hare
When she thinks that Phil is in it.

Chorus:
Oh, Mary, you're contrary –
Come in and bar the door;
What's that acufflin? Phil, you ruffian;
Sure I knew he'd come, asthore.
She's been settin' there and frettin',
But now her grievin's o'er
And the singin' will be ringing
In her heart once more.

29. No More of Yer Golfin' for Me

Musical arrangement by Houston Collisson

Through life I have played all the games that one can, At foot-ball I've played on the good Gael-ic plan, You may miss the ball, but you must kick the man, Or else it won't count to your score. At crick-et they nev-er knew what I'd be at, My ve-ry first welt laid the bowl-er out flat, As they had-n't an-oth-er I car-ried my bat While they car-ried him home on a door.

Chorus Golf! Golf! Car-ry me off, Bu-ry me down by the sea The put-ters may put, still I'll not stir a fut, No more o' yer Golf-in' for me.

I'm an old-fashioned dog to be larnin' new tricks,
But Murphy came round wid two bags full o' sticks,
At hockey you've one club, but here you have six,
And that's a remarkable thing.
Then Murphy drove off the wee ball, oh! Begor!
It rose through the air, till it looked like a star,
The head of my driver'd have gone just as far,
If it hadn't been tied with a string.

Chorus: Golf! Golf! Carry me off!
Bury me down by the sea.
The drivers may drive, but dead or alive,
No more o' yer golfin' for me.

When I got to the bunker, of clubs I'd just two,
But one was a brass wan, sez I, 'That'll do,
If the ball won't go over, I'll make it go through.'
So I slash'd and I hammer'd away.
Then Murphy came up, and sez he, 'Ain't it grand.'
Says I, 'It's a game I don't quite understand,
How much do they give here for shovellin' sand?
I'd like to get on by the day.'

Chorus: Golf! Golf! Carry me off!
Bury me down by the sea.
The lofters may loft,
Still my sleep shall be soft,
No more o' yer golfin' for me.

While I stood on the green, I heard some one cry 'Four'.
I paid no attention – that wasn't my score,
I had done the nine holes in two hundred or more,
When a ball hit the back of my head.
With Maguire it's always a blow for a blow,
I had just one club left – as I wheeled on my foe,
'Twas a beautiful lady, Begor! 'Twas no go,
'Did you see where the ball fell?' she said.

Spoken: 'Did I see?'
   'No! I hadn't seen it exactly, but I understood it was somewhere adjacent. In fact to the best of my incapacity it was somewhere contagious.'
   I was goin' to pick it up and give it to her, when she said: 'Oh! don't touch it. That's a lovely lie!'
   Of course, when she said that, I saw she knew all about my broken head, so I told her how I'd laid off to give her a welt across the face.
   That made us quite friendly at once, so I took her out of the firing line for a bit and axed her if we could not make a match of it.
   She said her match was Colonel Bogey!
   'Oh! thim soldiers. We ceevilians don't have a chance!'

Chorus: Golf! Golf! Carry me off!
Bury me down by the sea.
All the wurrld may go
To 'Old Bogey!' but oh!
No more o' yer golfin' for me.

30. The Darlin' Girl from Clare

Written and composed by Percy French

We were sit-tin' on the wall up-on a Sun-day To watch the girls go by, And think-in' we'd be mar-rit to one one day When Kate Flynn caught our eye. Oh, man, she was the mak-in's of a fai - ry And it made each 'boy-o swear! There's not one girl in the wide, wide world, Like the girl from the Coun-ty Clare! And ev - 'ry man had got the fin-est plan, You ev-er see now, Bar-rin' me now, Ev - 'ry day there's one of them would say, That she'll a-gree now, You'll see now, All night they'd fight, As to which o' them was right, In the col-our of her eyes and hair, But not a word from me was ev-er heard a-bout the dar-ling girl from Clare!

Says Fagin, "'Tis the father I'll be plazin',
I'll tell him of the land I've tilled,
I'll tell him of the cattle I have grazin'
And the house I mean to build;
And whin he sees the "arable" and "pasture"
And the fat stock feedin' there,
An' the hens an' the chickens,
Ye may go to the dickens
For the girl from the County Clare.'

Sez Sharkey, 'She'll be coming to the shop
To buy some sort of thing,   [there
I'll ax her if she has a mind to stop there,
And should I buy the ring.
An' whin she sees the curtains on the
An' the old clock on the stair   [window
Keepin' time to the minit,
No one else will be in it
With the darling girl from Clare!'

Chorus:
So every man had got the finest plan
Ye ever see now – barrin' me now,
Ev'ry day there's one of them would say
That she'll agree now – you'll see now
*Thinks I, 'Well then now
Though I haven't ere a cow
Of brass I've got my share,
And so I know the way they ought to go
About the darlin' girl from Clare.'

Chorus:
So every man had got the finest plan
Ye ever see now – barrin' me now,
Ev'ry day there's one of them would say
That she'll agree now – you'll see now
Thinks I, 'Ye may stop
Till yer dead in yer shop,
An' not a hair she'll care,
Wid all yer gold
Ye'll never hold a hold
Upon the darlin' girl from Clare.'

I never said a single word about her,
But I met the girl that day,
I told her I could never live widout her,
An' what had she to say?
She said that I might go and see her father:
I met him then and there,
An' in less than an hour
We were fightin' for the dower
Of the darlin' girl from Clare!

Chorus: So every man had got the finest plan
Ye ever see now – barrin' me now,
Ev'ry day there's one of them would say
That she'll agree now – you'll see now
But late last night
When the moon was bright
I axed her if she'd share
Me joy an' me sorra' –
An' begorra! on tomorra'
I'll be married to the girl from Clare.'

* Original lines here were:
  Thinks I to meself
  Though I haven't got the pelf

31. Pretendy Land

Music by J. A. Robertson

Where fairies live in a lovely wood,
Not bad fairies, nor yet too good,
We'll play with Little Red Riding Hood,
And, also with Little Boy Blue,
Where nobody's nasty and nobody's old,
And nobody's ever as good as gold,
And 'though you never do what you are
Yet nobody's cross with you.   [told

Over the Blanket billow, over the Bolster strand,
Both eyes must close e're my baby goes
Away to Pretendy Land,
Over the Hills of Pillow,
Wandering hand in hand.
Not a sigh! Not a sound!
Ah! baby has found
Her way to Pretendy Land.

32. Mrs Brady

Music by Houston Collisson

Ould Brady's gone to glo-ry and the wid-da has the land, And as she's good to look at, you can ea-sy un-der-stand, That el-i-gi-ble suit-ors from the town of Ath-en-ry, Put on their best em-bel-lish-ments and thought they'd have a try. Jim Flynn the sta-tion mas-ter's son, Tho' not in Bra-dy's set, Was kind e-nough to say to her one eve-ning when they met: 'Mis-sus Bra-dy! Just a whis-per! To your mourn-ing bid a-dieu! I know a fine young gen-tle-man Who'd not ob-ject to you, My fam-i-ly may cut me, But you've brass e-nough for two' 'I know who has the brass' says Mis-sus Bra-dy 'You've brass e-nough for three', says Mis-sus Bra - dy.

Pat Dempsey heard that Jimmy had been sent against the wall;
Says Pat, 'It's not gentility the widda wants at all.
But pity is akin to love, as everybody knows.
I'll tell her how I've got no girl to wash or mend my clothes.'
He dressed up like a scarecrow that across a field was hung,
And this was the come-hither that came slipping off his tongue.

Chorus: 'Mrs Brady, just a whisper!
I'd be glad to marry you
For indeed I've none to help me
With the work I have to do;
And the victuals that they cook me
I can neither chop nor chew.'
'I would not suit the place,' says Mrs Brady,
'I'd never do the work,' says Mrs Brady.

Then little Francis Fogarty said, 'Women, old and young,
Have always been deluthered by the civil-spoken tongue;
I'll tell her that her cheeks are like the summer rose in bloom,
Her eyes are like two diamonds, and her breath is sweet perfume.'
So off her goes to call on her, all flattery and lies,
And this was how he started in to carry off his prize.

Chorus: 'Mrs Brady, just a whisper!
There is none as fair as you,
Your face is like the dawn o' day.
Your lips are honey dew;
I'm certain you're an angel,
And it is from heaven you flew.'
'I believe you're off your head,' says Mrs Brady,
'You ought to see the vet,' says Mrs Brady.

When Flynn, who keeps the grocer's shop, and owns a bit o' land,
Came home and heard how Pat had got the back of Mary's hand,
Says he, 'Myself and Mary has been friends through thick and thin,'
So he put on all his Sunday clothes, and barbarised his chin;
He called on her that morning, she was very sweet and kind,
And this was how he hinted at the thoughts were in his mind:

Chorus: 'Mrs Brady, just a whisper!
Sure I don't know how to woo;
But I've got a growin' business,
And I've love enough for two;
To name the happy day,
And would tomorrow mornin' do?'
'Why not this afternoon?' says Mrs Brady,
'There's danger in delay!' says Mrs Brady.

33. Flaherty's Drake

Composed by Percy French on traditional tune

Oh I've come here be-fore ye, to tell ye a sto-ry, At the nar-ra-tive go-ry, your heart it will quake, For this is the his-to-ry, chock full of mys-te-ry, Of the black mur-der of Fla-her-ty's Drake. Now when Fla-her-ty died, he called me to his side, Says he, 'This di-vide of the farm I'll make, The house goes to Bid-dy, she's hon-est and stid-dy, And you'll take the stock, that's four ducks and a drake.'

Refrain

Quack, quack, quack went the ducks up-on his track, As they fol-lowed him down to the shore, They may quack, quack, quack, but he's nev-er com-ing back, He is nev-er com-ing back no more.

That night when in bed
In the loft overhead
The door of the shed
Gave a sort of a crake –
'Get up man!' says Biddy –
That's Flaherty's widdy –
'I think 'tis the voice of Ned Flaherty's drake.'

Now with that remark
I leapt up in the dark,
And ran like a lark
To the shore of the lake;
And there 'twas I found it,
Its four wives around it;
Some blackguard had drowned
Ned Flaherty's drake.   *Chorus:*

I made such a din
That the neighbours came in:
Says Councillor Flynn:
'Depositors I'll take
Build up a large fire
And then we'll enquire
What caused the demayse of Ned Flaherty's drake.'
When the coroner sat
On the bird, says he: 'Pat,
'Tis tender and fat
What a meal it would make.'
And then, never mindin'
The tears my eyes blindin',
They roasted and dined on
Ned Flaherty's drake.   *Chorus:*

34. The Mary Ann McHugh

Composed by Percy French, based on the old tune 'Limerick is beautiful'
Completed by James N. Healy (1982)

Come all ye lads who plough the seas, and al - so seize the plough The cruise of a can-al boat I am tell-ing to ye now It was the Ma - ry Ann mc Hugh that braved the an-gry surf And bore a-way from Mul - lin-gar with a ter-ri-ble load of turf. And the

63

cap - tain's name was Duff   His man - ners they were rough   But
ev - 'ry cape and head - land by   it's Christ-ian name he knew.   And he
is - sued this com - mand   'keep her well in sight of land   'Till we
make the port of Dub - lin in   the Ma - ry Ann Mc Hugh.'

The engine was of one horse-power; propelled wid a black-thorn stick,
Wid the wind astarn, and filled with corn, the horse went a terrible lick.
We worked her round the Hill o' Down, and then Kilcock we passed,
And when we seen John Flynn's Shebeen, we cried out 'Land at Last'.

But the captain, Jamesy Duff,
Cried, 'Luff! ye lubbers, luff!
And don't put in near Johnny Flynn
Whatever else ye do.
Last time we passed his door
We forgot to pay his score,
So he's got the polis watching for the Mary Ann McHugh.'

Then up and spake an old sailor who had sailed the Irish sea.
'I pray thee put into yonder port or the crew will mutinee:
To put to sea with the boy and me is a cruel thing, I think,
With water, water everywhere, and never a drop o' drink!'

But the captain, Jamesy Duff,
Cried, 'Enough, my lad, enough!'
No man before the mast shall ever tell me what to do.
Clap on all sail at wance,
For that's our only chance,
To keep from debt and danger in the Mary Ann McHugh.'

With anxious hearts the vessel starts upon her altered course,
The wind and waves they lashed the shore, and the pilot lashed the horse,
But all in vain – beneath the strain the rope began to part,
And she ran aground on a lump of coal that wasn't put down in the chart.

And the captain, Jamesy Duff,
He caught me such a cuff,
And then he said, 'Go heave the lead,' while the flag at half-mast flew,
But I had enough
Of the tyrant, Jamesy Duff,
So I heaved the lead at his head and fled from the Mary Ann McHugh.

35. The Kerry Courting

From 'The Rose of Tralee', an Irish Song-Cycle
by Percy French and Houston Collisson

Oh Ma-ry it's time ye were mar-ried I don't say yer much of a catch Wid

nev-er a pound in the bank I'll be bound no boy will be lift-in' the latch But

boys are mys-te-ri-ous creat-ures and when one is cra-zy to wed A

girl might bring him to give her the ring Be-fore he got right in his head For they

call you the 'Rose o' Tra-lee' It's all ve-ry pret-ty to be A

beaut-i-ful rose, But Lord on-ly knows who'll mar-ry the 'Rose o' Tra-lee' D'ye see? Who'll

mar-ry the 'Rose o' Tra-lee'. Still Jan-ey Del-a-ney got mar-ried Al-

-tho' she looks two ways at once And Car-rot-ty Peg with the twist in her leg So I'm

think-in' ye might have a chance of course thim two fair-ies had mon-ey That

gave them a bit of a push But all that you've got in the crock-er-y pot Would-n't

whis-tle a boy off the bush And they call ye the 'Rose o' Tra-lee' It's

all ve-ry pret-ty to be A beaut-i-ful rose, But Lord on-ly knows who'll

mar-ry the 'Rose o' Tra-lee' D'ye see? Who'll mar-ry the 'Rose o' Tra-lee.'

36. A Sailor Courted a Farmer's Daughter

Parody of old ballad: Percy French

Oh! A sail-or court-ed a far-mer's daugh-ter, who lived con-ta-gious to the Isle of

Man. With war-bling mel-o-dies he did be-sought her, to mar-ry

him be-fore she'd mar-ry an-y oth-er sort of a kind of a man. But the far-mer's

daugh-ter had great po-ses-sions, A sil-ver tay - pot and two pounds in

gold, And said she, 'Would yer mar-ry me, me bold salt wa-ter sea

sail-or, If I threw them in-to the o-cean cold.' Oh! said he, 'I'll

mar-ry you me heart's en-chant-ment, If you had noth-ing but your fa-ther's

curse.' So she made up a bun-dle of all her grand po-

-ses - sions, and threw them in-ter the wa-ter; That ends that

verse. But the sail-or he could swim like a duck-ling, So in-to the

'wa-ter he dived down deep be-low, Got hold of the bun-dle and swum a-way

chuck-ling, To think of the times he'd be hav-ing when he land-ed down in Bal-lin-as-

-loe. But the far-mer's daugh-ter was kil't with the laugh-in', To think of the

bun-dle she made out of the stone. Oh! A sail-or cour-ted a far-mer's

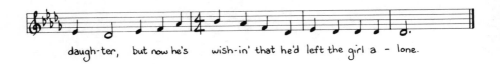

daugh-ter, but now he's wish-in' that he'd left the girl a - lone.

37. Tullinahaw

Music: traditional, arranged by Houston Collisson

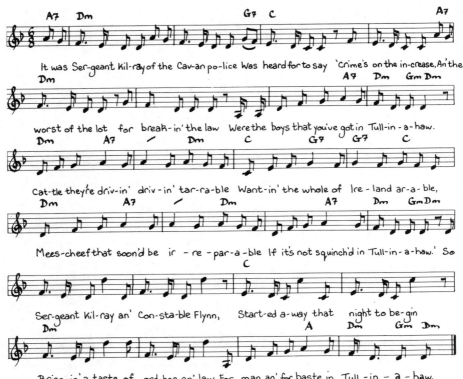

It was Ser-geant Kil-ray of the Cav-an po-lice Was heard for to say 'Crime's on the in-crease, An' the
worst of the lot for break-in' the law Were the boys that you've got in Tull-in-a-haw.
Cat-tle they're driv-in' driv-in' tar-ra-ble Want-in' the whole of Ire-land ar-a-ble,
Mees-cheef that soon'd be ir - re - par-a-ble If it's not squinch'd in Tull-in-a-haw.' So
Ser-geant Kil-ray an' Con-sta-ble Flynn, Start-ed a-way that night to be-gin
Bring-in' a taste of ord-her an' law For man an' for baste in Tull-in-a-haw.

Oh they lay by the wall an' they kep' wide awake
'Till they saw a man haulin' a cow in the lake,
'Honest man, tell me now is that cow all your own?'
'Is it me own a cow that's all skin and bone?
Sure she belongs to Widda Geraghty
Home I was drivin' her from charity.'
'Tell me,' says Flynn – with some halarity,
'Why are you comin' from Tullinahaw?'
An' Sergeant Kilray was heard for to say,
'The case is suspeecious in ev-er-y way.'

68

And Flynn said he saw a breach of the law
In drivin' a cow from Tullinahaw.

Oh, the trial came on an' the prisoner swore
He was doin' a neighbourly act an' no more,
For the cow was no use and the Widda that day
Had give him a bob to take it away!
'Stop!' said the judge, 'You've made no case of it.
That is a lie, sir, on the face of it,
Perjury too there's ev'ry trace of it,
Years they'll miss you in Tullinahaw.'
And Sergeant Kilray and Constable Flynn,
They made no delay in runnin' him in.
An' there for a year he sits in the straw
Lamentin' the grandeurs of Tullinahaw.

When they brought back the cow, says the Widda, 'Ochone!
How I wish them police would leave people alone,
For if I could have proved the ould reptile was drown'd
I'd ha' got compinsation – aye – nine or ten pound.
Instid of the money to help further me,
Here the ould baste is back to bother me,
Whin John comes out I know he'll murther me,
Gettin' him took in Tullinahaw.
An' Sergeant Kilray and Constable Flynn,
The both of them grey and elderly min,
Still tell how they brought back ordher an' law –
'Tis a different story in Tullinahaw!

38. The Emigrant's Letter

Music by Ernest Hastings

Dear Dan-ny I'm ta-kin' the pen in me hand To
tell you we're just out o' sight o' the land In the
grand Al-lan Li-ner We're sail-ing in style But I'm

I spoke to the captain – he won't turn her round,
And if I swum back I'd be apt to be drowned,
I'll stay where I am, for the diet is great
The best of combustibles piled on me plate.
But though it is 'Sumpchus', I'd swop the whole lot,
For the ould wooden spoon and the stirabout pot,
And Kitty foreninst me a-wettin' the tay
Where they're cuttin' the corn in Creeshla the day!

There's a woman on board who knows Katey by sight
So we talked of old times 'till they put out the light.
I'm to meet the good woman tomorra' on deck
And we'll talk about Katey from this to Quebec.
I know I'm no match for her – oh! not the leesht,
With her house and two cows, and her brother a preesht.
But the woman declares Katey's heart's on the say
And mine's back with Katey in Creeshla the day.

If Katey is courted by Patsey or Mick,
Put a word in for me with a lump of a stick,
Don't kill Patsey outright, he had no sort of chance,
But Mickey's a rogue you might murther at wance;
For Katey might think, as the longer she waits,
A boy in the hand is worth two in the States:
And she'll promise to honour, to love and obey
Some rover that's roamin' round Creeshla the day.

Goodbye to you, Dan, there's no more to be said,
And I think the salt wather's got into me head,
For it dreeps from me eyes when I call to me mind,
The friends and the Colleen I'm leaving behind.
But still she might wait, whin I bid her goodbye,
There was just the last taste of a tear in her eye,
And a break in her voice whin she said, 'You might stay,
But plaze God you'll come back to ould Creeshla some day.'

39. Kitty Gallagher

Written by Percy French

Oh I've court-ed man-y a one, And me heart has been un-done, So of-ten that ye'd think that it was gone o' me; But faith I know 'tis there Since I first was made a-ware of beau-ti-ful Miss kit-ty's phy-si-on-o-my. Talk of Ve-nus! she was no way her su-per-i-or Talk of Li-ly Lang-try! she would sing un-com-mon small! Ma-ry Ann McGill-i-gan was ev-'ry way in-fer-i-or Pret-ty Kit-ty Gal-lagh-er's the dar-lin' of them all.

Chorus

Pret-ty kit-ty Gal-lagh-er, sure and I could swal-low her, She'd be cream and su-gar in me tay: Oh! Pret-ty kit-ty Gal-lagh-er, faith, and I could fol-low her, O-ver all the world and a-way.

I fought the whole townland,
And the Finn McCool brass band,
Who thought they had a sort of prior claim to her;
But with me kippeen in me hand,
Faith, I made them understand
That Brady was the man to give a name to her.
Mick McCoogan would persuade me to surrender her,

72

Now he finds it difficult to use a brush and comb,
I dunno if his head or if his heart is now the tenderer.
We fought for pretty Kitty till the cows were coming home.
Chorus:

Of no man was I afraid,
But they made an ambuscade;
A course that would have paralysed Napoleon:
But before they laid me out
Faith, I caught them many a clout,
You wouldn't find a head but was a holey 'un!
When Miss Kitty seen the broken-headed regiment,
Paradin' out in front of her and askin' her to wife,
Kneelin' down beside me corp the duck of diamonds said she meant
To take the man they murdered and that brought me back to life!
Chorus:

40. Flanagan's Flying Machine

Music by W. H. Collisson

'Twas Flan-a-gan found out the sec-ret of flight And made such a per-fect af-fair That Far-man and Bler-i-ot, Lath-am and White Pro-claim'd him the King of the Air. And, mind you, I think he de-serv'd his suc-cess For real-ly he work'd ve-ry hard Six days out of sev-en his pri-vate ad-dress Was the hos-pit-al ac-ci-dent ward! But soon he was safe and ser-ene And

73

ev-e-ry day could be seen   By ad-mir-ing crowds   Lep-pin'

ov-er the clouds In his mar-vel-lous fly-ing ma-chine,   His

mar-vel-lous fly-ing ma-chine.

Said the Kaiser, 'On Britain I'm going to pounce
Like a terrier dog on a rat.'
Said his officers, 'Do, and you'll get the grand bounce,
For you're talking too much through your hat.'
Said the Kaiser, 'There's nothing on earth you'll allow
My army and fleet can defy.'
Said his officers, 'Nothin' on earth, sire, but how
About something up there in the sky?'
Said the Kaiser, 'I know what you mean
Though, faith!, I'd forgotten it clean,
The war is postponed
While the atmosphere's owned
By Flanagan's flying machine.'

Mrs Bryan was bringing her baby along
To be christened Patricia Kathleen,
When over the hill, on its way to Hong Kong
Came Flanagan's flying machine.
Says poor Mrs Bryan, 'Oh! was that a bat,
Or a big dragon fly that I seen?'
Says Bryan, 'Och, woman, go 'long out o' that
It was Flanagan's flying machine.'
Oh, Flanagan's flyin' machine!
When she handed his riv'rence the wean
'Twas no wonder he smiled,
When he said, 'Name this child,'
She said, 'Flanagan's flyin' machine.'

The King and the Queen were enjoyin' a drive,
When their motor broke down by the way;
And the Queen said, 'Oh Murther!
We'll never arrive
In time for me afthernoon tay.'
Then Tim came along in his aeroplane

74

And, whoosin' them up in the air,
Had the two of them back in Balmoral again
Wid a cuple of minutes to spare.
And the King he remarked to the Queen,
'Was iver the like of it seen?
Tim! ye Divil,' he said,
'Take the crown oft my head,
But give me yer flying machine.'

41. Who Said the Hook Never Hurted the Worms?

From 'Freda and the Fairies': music by Caroline Maude

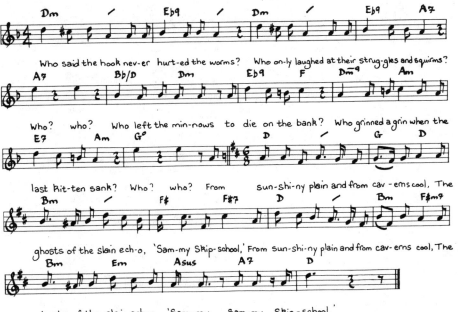

Who shot the pigeon they baked in a pie?
Who pulled the wings off a poor little fly?
Who? Who?
Who chased and frightened a poor little lamb?
Who broke the window, and who stole the jam?
Who? Who?
From sunshiny plain and from caverns cool,
The ghosts of the slain echo,
'Sammy skip-school'.

42. I Fought a Fierce Hyena

From 'Freda and the Fairies': music by Caroline Maude

I've fought a fierce hy – e – na, He was just as high as high! So have I, so have I! Mine was high-er than the sky. On-ly fan-cy kill-ing some-thing that was high-er than the sky. I have killed a hip-per- -pot-o-mus, Much big-ger than a wall. Is that all? that was small, Mine was near-ly twice as tall. Just fan-cy kill-ing some-thing that was near-ly twice as tall. I know you don't be-lieve me, That is plain e-nough to see, But once I killed a bee-tle, And I've of-ten killed a bee. They know we don't be-lieve them, That is plain e-nough to see, But once they killed a bee-tle, And they've of-ten killed a bee.

Sammy:	I killed a dreadful dragon
	That drank up the Forth of Firth.
Freda:	So did mine, so did mine!
	He just swallowed up the earth.
Chorus:	Only fancy killing something that could swallow up the earth.
Sammy:	I have killed a great sea-serpent,
	Yes, I killed it with an axe.
Freda:	I killed six, with some bricks
	And a bit of cobbler's wax.
Chorus:	How clever to kill serpents with a bit of cobbler's wax.
Both:	I know you don't believe me, etc.
Sammy:	I only use a pop-gun
	When I kill a tiger-cat.
Freda:	I killed mine with some twine –
	Just about as long as that.
Chorus:	Killing tiger-cats with pop-guns and a string as long as that.
Sammy:	I was fishing off an ice-berg,
	And I caught an 'normous whale.
Freda:	I caught five, all alive,
	And I keep them in a pail.
Chorus:	How wonderful to keep 'normous fishes in a pail.
Both:	I know you don't believe me, etc.

43. The Killyran Wrackers

Music: first half by Percy French Completed by James N. Healy (1982)

Now this is the sto-ry of the boys who left our vil-lage Un-der Kit Ma-gor-ey that mil-it-a-ry man. Some they go for glo-ry, and some they go for pil-lage, And the lat-ter was the mot-ive with the boys of kill-y-ran. But from the field of glo-ry There came an-oth-er sto-ry And Col-onel kit Ma-gor-ey gave me to un-der-stand At Al-ma, Ba-la-

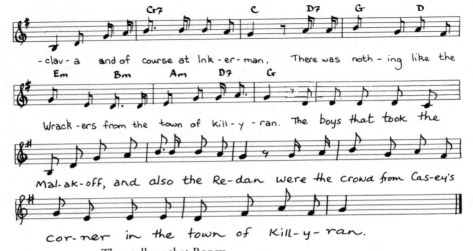

-clav-a and of course at Ink-er-man, There was noth-ing like the
Wrack-ers from the town of kill-y-ran. The boys that took the
Mal-ak-off, and also the Re-dan were the crowd from Cas-ey's
cor-ner in the town of Kill-y-ran.

They tell me that Boney,
At Waterloo was winning,
And so he would have, only the Prussians lent a hand,
Says Boney, 'Alone I
Would send the Britons spinning,
But I cannot stand the music of that Blucher's German Band!'

But from the field of glory
There came another story
And Colonel Kit Magorey
Gave me to understan'
Says Boneyparte, 'My veterans have done what mortals can
But they couldn't face the Wrackers from the town of Killyran!
It's not that Sepoy General who spoilt my finest plan,
It's that regiment of ruffians from the town of Killyran!'

They tell me that Great Britain
Is soon to be undone,
In the *Daily Mail* 'tis written
And so it must be true.
A great big German army comes annihilating London,
While 'Bobs'* and all his regulars are beaten black and blue.

But from the field of glory
Will come another story
And Colonel Kit Magorey
Gives me to understan'
No foe will ever face us, if only in the van
Is that mob of malefactors from the town of Killyran.
And if the Kaiser ever tries the flame of war to fan,
Berlin will be bombarded by the Boys of Killyran.

* Roberts, the English military hero of the Boer War.

44. Larry Mick McGarry

Music by Percy French

Oh, Larry played old Harry
With the girls about the place,
At the dancin' they'd be glancin'
At the features of his face,
But he never would endeavour
To be lover-like until
Mary Carey, she's a fairy,
Had him goin' like a mill.

Chorus: Titheryah the doodle ah
He met her in the street,
Titheryah the doodle ah
Sez he, 'Yer lookin' sweet.
A walk an' a talk wid you
I think would be a treat.'
But all he got from Mary was,
'Good morning!'

The dancin' down at Clancy's
Brought in all the neighbourhood,
Though the roof wasn't waterproof,
The floor was fairly good;
An' Larry Mick McGarry
He could handle well the leg,
But Mary, light an' airy,
Oh, she took him down a peg.

Chorus: Titheryah the doodle ah
She footed it wid Flynn
Titheryah the doodle ah
An' all the other min.
But Larry Mick McGarry
Oh! he hadn't a look in,
Faith, he had to go and find her
In the morning.

Oh, she taught him till she brought him
Up to where she had designed
Sez Larry, 'Will ye marry me?'
Sez she, 'I wouldn't mind.'
He kissed her an' carissed her
Which is quite the proper thing
Then together, hell for leather
They were off to buy a ring.

Chorus: Titheryah the doodle ah
'No marryin',' sez you,
Titheryah the doodle ah
Ye may escape the 'flu
Wait till you meet yer mate
An' all there is to do
Is to go an' buy the licence
In the morning.